EVERYDAY QUESTIONS FOR SUCCESS

365 POWERFUL QUESTIONS TO INSPIRE BUSINESS AND PERSONAL GROWTH

LINDA DELUCA

EVERYDAY QUESTIONS FOR SUCCESS
365 Powerful Questions To Inspire
Business And Personal Growth

ISBN-13: 978-1547097944
ISBN-10: 1547097949

Published by Azione Scopo Publishing www.azionescopopublishing.com

Cover design by MY Designs, my-designs.net
Published in the United States of America

Created with Vellum

INTRODUCTION

WHAT'S IT ABOUT?

The ultimate actionable strategy for business and personal growth is powerful questioning.

Long or short, complex or simple, a powerful question evokes discovery and insight, clarity and commitment, and innovation and action. Asking the right question at the right time can change everything.

If you've ever witnessed artful questioning, you know the power it holds. And if you've ever wished you could have that power, now's your chance.

Everyday Questions For Success gives you a collection of 365 questions curated over decades of consulting and coaching in organizations large and small.

Clarity and growth come with taking action, not just thinking. These questions are intended to inspire action with purpose.

WHO SHOULD READ THIS BOOK?

This book is for you - the leader, manager, coach, consultant, independent freelancer, entrepreneur, trainer, or aspiring professional looking for an actionable strategy to become better at what you do. You already have a great deal of knowledge. Let's turn that knowledge into wisdom by digging deeper and uncovering the next big thing for you.

The better you get at asking questions; the better you'll be at answering them.

WHAT'S THE BEST APPROACH?

There are three ways to take advantage of the content of Everyday Questions For Success:

1. One Question Every Day.

In PART ONE (365 Daily Questions) there is a list of 365 questions for you to follow through the course of a year. Make it a daily prompt to encourage creativity and productivity.

Over time you may find you'll use the same 10 or 20 questions because of the situations you are in or your style. I recommend highlighting your favorite 10 or 20 for easy reference.

Every once in a while, try randomly selecting a different question and see what happens. It will keep you from being too predictable and from getting into a rut.

2. Questions By Topic

PART TWO includes questions grouped by situation or topic. If you have a decision to make, there is a list of helpful questions to help. Faced with a difficult conversation? There's a section for that too. Go to this section when you need to dive deeper into one particular topic.

3. Randomly Select A Question.

Identify a random number between 1 and 365. Go to that question and answer it. Even if you select the same questions each time, the context in which you'll be asking the question will change.

The Ultimate Actionable Strategy

Questions are used to gain clarity and understanding. The power you'll experience ultimately resides in the action it inspires.

My challenge to you: after you answer a question or group of questions fully, ask the ultimate question:

What will you do?

This book and my entire body of work are dedicated to helping people like you grow themselves and their businesses so they can deliver their best work - everyday.

Don't forget to pick up your **bonus thank you gift** at the end of the book!

Thanks for reading.

Linda DeLuca

PART I
EVERYDAY QUESTIONS

Following is a list of 365 questions for you to ask yourself or your team.

Some questions are presented in a logical order while others are random. This intentional design will allow your thoughts to flow, but will challenge you before you get comfortable.

The goal is to help you shift perspective, think deeply, and inspire you to do your best work everyday.

DAILY QUESTIONS 01 - 31

1. What is this year's guidepost?
2. How will this impact those important to you?
3. What are you afraid of?
4. What's important here?
5. Does it make you happy?
6. What do you want?
7. What is the better version of you?
8. What's it going to take to put you in the center of your own life?
9. What 10 books have you read that had significant impact for you personally or professionally?
10. How do you describe success in this situation?
11. If you could go back and talk to your younger self, what would you like her/him to know?
12. If there were no constraints, what would you do? If you suspended doubt and worry, what action would you take?
13. What are you ready to commit to right now?

14. What are you truly committed to?
15. What is really important to you - rather than merely urgent? What is your underlying purpose here?
16. When was the last time you lost track of time? What were you doing at the time?
17. What are the three most important elements of a life filled with joy?
18. Why do you work?
19. What are your top three pet peeves?
20. What drains your energy?
21. What emotion do you least want to feel?
22. What emotion do you most want to feel?
23. What energizes you?
24. What's the most important thing you learned from your parents?
25. What unique contribution can you make?
26. How would you rate / describe your satisfaction with respect to: finances? Is that what you want? If not, what do you want to be different here?
27. What's your vision of your lifestyle in 5 / 10 / 15 years?
28. What do you need to be doing 6 months / 1 year / 5 years before your vision becomes a reality?
29. What do you need to believe in order to turn your vision into reality?
30. What do you need to have done to turn your vision into reality?
31. What do you need to know to turn your vision into reality?

DAILY QUESTIONS 32 - 59

1. What will it take to make your vision a reality?
2. What's your vision of your professional future in 5 / 10 / 15 years?
3. How would you rate / describe your satisfaction with respect to: work? Is that what you want? If not, what do you want to be different here?
4. What type of things can you do to close the gap? Reduce the difference?
5. How would you rate / describe your satisfaction with respect to: family? Is that what you want? If not, what do you want to be different here?
6. How would you rate / describe your satisfaction with respect to: friends/social? Is that what you want? If not, what do you want to be different here?
7. How would you rate / describe your satisfaction with respect to: health? Is that what you want? If not, what do you want to be different here?
8. How would you rate / describe your satisfaction with

respect to: spirituality? Is that what you want? If not, what do you want to be different here?

9. What things do you like or dislike in each area of your life/business?
10. What are you doing now to shape your life tomorrow?
11. What's missing from this picture so far?
12. What 5 items would you put on your bucket list?
13. Where are you along your plan?
14. What bothers you most in the world?
15. What would you do if you knew you could not fail?
16. What's your biggest hope or dream?
17. What do you really want - specifically?
18. How can you make what you want achievable?
19. How will things (your life, your interactions, your thoughts, your behaviors) be different once you have what you want?
20. How will you know when you've got what you want?
21. If you could do (whatever you've regretted) over, what would be different?
22. What do you regret? How can you avoid that specific regret in the future?
23. What makes you uncomfortable? Is there something to learn from that?
24. What do you think will happen if you say no to this request?
25. What's the cascading effect of saying no?
26. What's the cascading effect of saying yes?
27. What do you want to be different next (week / quarter / year)?
28. What do you need to be thinking / doing / feeling / saying differently to make that a reality?

DAILY QUESTIONS 60-90

1. How do you want them to behave differently?
2. Why don't you say something?
3. Why don't you do something?
4. What's the elephant in the room for this meeting / conversation / project / decision?
5. How are you measuring success?
6. Is there a better way to measure success or progress?
7. What has changed since you chose that measure of success? Is it still relevant?
8. What are you feeling right now?
9. What triggered this feeling?
10. Why do you feel this way?
11. What recurring thoughts are you having?
12. How are these thoughts impacting your decision-making, behavior, focus, productivity, or happiness?
13. What do you know so far about the situation?
14. What do you still need to know about the situation?
15. What opportunities can you see in your situation?

16. What resources can you call on to help?
17. What's the business impact of this situation?
18. What do you wish you had said in that difficult conversation?
19. What is the most difficult conversation you've had in your professional life?
20. What are your assumptions?
21. What are your choices?
22. What can you learn from this situation so far?
23. What matters most to you in this situation?
24. What five individuals do you spend the most time with?
25. What five individuals do you want to spend more time with?
26. Is this a need or a want?
27. Where do you need to focus your energy right now ?
28. What are you avoiding?
29. What can you do right now, today, to move closer to achieving your goal?
30. What's outside your control?
31. What's within your control?

DAILY QUESTIONS 91 - 120

1. Are you drained or energized by this?
2. How will you reduce the negative impact of your most prominent weakness in your work / conversations / relationships?
3. What are you tolerating in your professional life right now?
4. What do other people experience as your top character strength?
5. What's frustrating you right now?
6. What's keeping you from delivering your best work everyday?
7. What's the biggest mistake you've ever made, and why was that a good thing?
8. What's your process for deciding whether or not to take on a project?
9. What's your weakness?
10. Where could you use this skill in the future?

11. Who's your mentor? What qualities do you admire most in them?
12. Are your thoughts / feelings / or actions keeping you from succeeding?
13. What is your superpower?
14. What's your top character strength?
15. Are you being overly positive about this?
16. How do you help co-workers / clients / customers?
17. How do you want this situation to be different from prior situations?
18. What 10 books will you read this year to stay relevant?
19. What do you need to do right now?
20. What do you need to know?
21. What has worked for you in the past in similar situations?
22. What problems do you solve?
23. What relevant qualities and skills do you already have and how can you apply them to the current situation?
24. Who's one or two steps ahead that you can learn from?
25. Are you being overly negative about this?
26. If we're sitting here a year from now celebrating something huge, what would it be?
27. What would your role model do in this situation?
28. What are you not telling your boss / partner that they need to know?
29. What are you not admitting in this situation?
30. What have you been doing automatically, which may need reexamined?

DAILY QUESTIONS 121 - 150

1. What do you expect from this?
2. What do you want from this?
3. When have you been in a similar situation?
4. What are you responsible for?
5. What impact has this meant for others at work?
6. What matters most to you in this moment?
7. Who did you make a genuine connection with today?
8. What do you believe about yourself in this situation?
9. What would help sustain positive momentum?
10. What learning format best suits your style or preference?
11. What would you have changed about the experience?
12. What are you tolerating in your personal life right now?
13. What biases are you depending on?
14. What impact has this had for you?
15. What's your worst habit?
16. Who are you avoiding and why?
17. If you could have one do-over, what would it be?

18. What about yourself do you loath?
19. What are you holding onto (ideas/things/beliefs/habits) that no longer serve you?
20. What are your perceptions on why this situation has occurred?
21. What aren't you struggling with that you should be? (This is about growth - we need struggle to grow but we need to struggle with the right thing).
22. What can we do to rectify the situation?
23. What do you need to be different in order to move forward on this matter?
24. What's a habit you're trying to adopt right now?
25. What's the best creative advice you've ever been given?
26. Who's one or two steps behind that you can help?
27. Is there anything that you are not noticing that you need to pay attention to? If you were an objective observer of yourself, what would you now say?
28. What do you believe that limits you? What assumptions have you been making that are no longer valid?
29. What is easier now?
30. What is faster now?

DAILY QUESTIONS 151 - 181

1. What is still challenging?
2. What was working but is not longer?
3. What's not working?
4. What's possible?
5. What's really happening?
6. How can you listen more to your inner wisdom?
7. What's working?
8. What matters most to you in your overall career/business?
9. Who in your professional life can you count on to provide you with honest, constructive feedback?
10. How will you experience your business relationships and conversations one year form now if you do nothing to change or improve them?
11. What do you need your boss / manager to know in order to be successful?
12. What do you need your partner to know in order to be successful?

13. What do we need more clarity about?
14. What's the cost in time, money, reputation, energy, or other resources?
15. What do you need from your accountability partner?
16. Who in your professional life can you count on to be a true accountability partner?
17. What's your preferred form of communication?
18. What's more important for this (project/situation) time or money?
19. What are the facts in this situation?
20. What dependencies does this project / decision / action have?
21. Why haven't you done this before?
22. What are all the possible ways of completing this task/project?
23. In what team role do you feel most confident?
24. What's more important for this (project/situation) people or process?
25. What's more important for this (project/situation) quality or quantity?
26. Do you feel secure in your current earning power?
27. If you won the lottery and didn't need to work, ho would you spend your time?
28. What resources do you need?
29. What information do you need to make this decision?
30. What area / skill may you be at risk of thinking you're better than you actually are?
31. What area / skill may you be at risk of thinking you're worse than you actually are?

DAILY QUESTIONS 182 - 212

1. How can your coach/mentor support you in taking the next step?
2. How would you describe your peers?
3. If you had a magic wand and could solve any world problem, what problem would you solve?
4. If you had to focus the rest of your life on one thing, what would it be?
5. Is there a critical deadline associated with this project/goal?
6. What are you missing in your life/work?
7. What do you and your peers have in common?
8. What do you need from your boss / manager to be successful?
9. What do you need from your partner to be successful?
10. What do you wish everyone would recognize in you? What strength / gift / wish?
11. What keeps you up at night?

12. What unique contribution can your coach/mentor make to help you move forward?
13. Are you basing your decision on current or past information?
14. Around whom do you feel most comfortable?
15. How can a trusted advisor assist with this situation?
16. How would you prioritize your options?
17. In what environment are you most comfortable?
18. In what situations are you most naturally yourself?
19. What are the possible solutions to address this situation or gap?
20. What behaviors or habits do you need to change?
21. What can you think, do, or feel to make this situation different?
22. What did you learn from the biggest mistake you ever made?
23. What do you want to be doing all day?
24. What gets you out of bed early on a weekend to do?
25. What knowledge do you need?
26. What makes you feel most confident?
27. What makes you lose track of time when you do it?
28. What words do people use to describe you when they introduce you to others?
29. What's emerging here for you? What new connections are you making?
30. What's the best approach to making this decision?
31. What's the part of your job you love the most?

DAILY QUESTIONS 213 - 243

1. About what topic(s) can you talk endlessly?
2. Are you happy with the way things are going? if not, what are you going to do about it? When?
3. Have you done this before? If so, what happened?
4. Is there a way to test-drive the opportunity?
5. Is there an easier way?
6. What are you most proud of?
7. What can you stop doing to make room for positive change?
8. What do others tell you is your greatest strength?
9. What do people come to you for?
10. What important choices are available to you now? In five years' time what decision will you be glad you had now made?
11. What most strongly sets you apart from your peers?
12. What unique ingredient do you contribute to everything you do that without you would be missed?

13. What would you like this to look like in three months' time?

14. What's the most useful thing you could do right now to take you where you want to go?

15. When do you need to make this decision?

16. Who are you becoming?

17. Are you moving in a direction of your choosing? If not, what do you choose to do about it? When?

18. What are your plans to manage the cost of implementing changes?

19. What changes do you need to initiate, and how will you initiate those changes?

20. What do you do better than anyone else?

21. What five words (adjectives) would you use to describe yourself?

22. What's unique about the way you do what you do (the way you achieve results)?

23. What evidence would you give to someone who doubted your interpretation?

24. Are you judging based on your own values or theirs?

25. How much time and energy will you devote to improving your communication skills?

26. What challenged you from what you've heard?

27. What had real meaning for you from what you've heard?

28. What surprised you from what you've heard?

29. How is sharing this information / opinion about someone else (who is not present) going to help them?

30. How will developing stronger communication skills help ease your conversational concerns?

31. What are you experiencing right now in your business conversations that causes you concern?

DAILY QUESTIONS 244 - 273

1. How do you think the other person views the situation?
2. What isn't being said that needs to be?
3. Are your expectations realistic?
4. Whose opinion matters in this situation?
5. What are they thinking, feeling, and wanting?
6. What are you having a hard time believing because of who's sharing the information?
7. If you viewed things from another person's point of view, what new information would that perspective give you?
8. How will this impact others?
9. How can you avoid discussing things you've already agree on and move onto the difficult conversations?
10. Who plays the supporting role to you as the hero? Who is your biggest fan?
11. What are you relying too heavily on? What have you anchored your opinion on?

12. Is this the right time for this conversation / project / action?
13. What do you think they should know without me telling them? Is that reasonable?
14. Is what I'm about to say helping to achieve our/my goal? Does it add value?
15. What if you stopped doing it?
16. What if you didn't do it?
17. When will you know that this approach is no longer working?
18. What does 'done' look like?
19. How much time should you spend planning versus doing in this situation?
20. What's in the way of getting this done?
21. What's not getting done?
22. Why did you make this decision? Is it still true?
23. What should you/your team be firm on?
24. What should you/your team be more open to?
25. What should you/your team do less of?
26. What should you/your team do more of?
27. What should you/your team learn how to do?
28. What should you/your team stop doing?
29. What should your/your team start doing?
30. Who has recently done this task/project successfully/unsuccessfully and how can you learn from them?

DAILY QUESTIONS 274 - 304

1. What's the problem you're trying to solve?
2. Why solve this problem now?
3. Are you listening to all contributors regardless of position / authority?
4. What's the most common question asked about this project/task/product/requirement?
5. How much money do you keep?
6. How much money do you save?
7. How much money do you earn?
8. Can you survive an unexpected financial burden of $500? $5,000? $50,000?
9. Do you have a financial plan for this quarter / year?
10. Do you know where every penny of your earned money goes each month?
11. How do you track your earnings and spending?
12. What are your detailed expected expenses for the coming 18 months?

13. What can you put in place to adhere to your financial plan?
14. Where in your business can you use a creative solution to avoid increasing your debt?
15. Are you realistically estimating the time / cost to complete this project / task?
16. How can you avoid sunk cost bias?
17. What resource is most at risk of running out?
18. What's the best that could happen?
19. What's the most likely outcome?
20. What's the worst that could happen?
21. What's keeping you busy?
22. What do you need to do differently to use your time more effectively?
23. What good will you do today?
24. What will you do to transform the 50,000 thoughts you have each day into mostly positive instead of the normal mostly negative?
25. What good have you done today?
26. Is the obstacle real or imagined?
27. What distracts you from your most important work?
28. What do you need them to know, in order to feel comfortable delegating this task to this person?
29. What energy are you putting in to achieving your goals?
30. What needs to happen in order for you to take that item off your plate / list?
31. What one thing can you remove from you to-do list - forever?

1. What project / task needs your undivided attention today?
2. What would you like to take off your 'plate' / 'responsibility list'?
3. Who needs your undivided attention today?
4. What can you do today to focus more on what's important and essential?
5. Do you have to be at this meeting or event?
6. If not now, when?
7. What do you spend too much time on that has little or no value?
8. What are you REALLY hungry for?
9. How else could you describe your behavior in this situation?
10. When might this scenario be appropriate?
11. What we think about today will create who we are tomorrow. Are you drawing in success? Or are you drawing in defeat?

12. If you could change one thing about yourself, what would it be?
13. Does the problem really lie in the action or in the way you feel about the action?
14. How exactly would you deal with the worst-case scenario? What are the exact steps you would take to get back from the worst-case scenario?
15. How is your public persona different from the real you?
16. In the worst-case scenario, what happens down the road?
17. In what circumstances are you most honest?
18. What are you struggling with that you shouldn't be?
19. What are your concerns and worries about the situation?
20. What do you think the next step could be?
21. What feedback will help you along the way?
22. What past events are you re-writing to appear more successful?
23. What past events do you want to avoid repeating?
24. What quality in others do you admire the most?
25. What structure and support do you need?
26. What was the best decision you ever made? Why?
27. What will be different now?
28. What will you do next?
29. What would you do if your job depended on the resolution of this problem?
30. What's your favorite thing to do in your free time?

DAILY QUESTIONS 335 - 365

1. What's within your power to change?
2. When considering this opportunity, do you feel expansive (feeling of something big, positive, exciting) or contractive (closed, small, limited)?
3. When you resolve this issue, what will be different?
4. Who's affected by this situation?
5. Why do you want to go out on your own?
6. Are you directing your thinking in a useful direction? What will be the most productive direction for your thinking?
7. Are your habitual behaviors productive in terms of what you now want?
8. Have you considered the most relevant information or are you only using what is easily available?
9. How will you know you've been successful in achieving your goal?
10. What about yourself do you love?

11. What are potential obstacles and how will you overcome them?
12. What are the possible payoffs for saying yes to this opportunity? Be specific.
13. What are you resisting?
14. What decisions have you made similar to this one? How can you learn from that to help you decide now?
15. What do you like best about yourself?
16. What do you need to acknowledge yourself for? What deserves celebration?
17. What will change?
18. What would it take for you to be your own strongest ally? How can you get out of your own way?
19. What's the most unique/quirkiest think about you?
20. What's your plan and when will you begin?
21. When should you stop asking others for input on decisions?
22. Who do you hear from the least?
23. Who do you hear from the most?
24. Who is the most stressed on the team?
25. Who on your team is overwhelmed?
26. Do you trust yourself?
27. If you were to receive an award, what would it be for?
28. Where are the bottlenecks in your business/process? Where is the work piled up?
29. What's the first step?
30. Who's impacted by this decision?
31. What action will make the greatest difference?

PART II
QUESTIONS BY TOPIC

Each of the listed topics includes questions to get you started. Often that's all we need to start a discussion, get unstuck, move forward toward success.

The same question, asked by a different person or in a different context, can bring new insight.

You'll find the topic lists include the 365 questions but also may include new questions.

Remember, questions are the ultimate actionable strategy. What will you do now?

BUSINESS

1. What's important here?
2. What are your assumptions?
3. How will this impact those important to you?
4. What are your choices?
5. What can you learn from this situation so far?
6. Where do you need to focus your energy right now?
7. What unique contribution can you make?
8. What is this year's guidepost?
9. What 10 books will you read this year to stay relevant?
10. What do you need to do right now?
11. What do you need to know?
12. Are you being overly negative about this?
13. Are you being overly positive about this?
14. What's your vision of your professional future in 5 / 10 / 15 years?
15. What will it take to make your vision a reality?
16. What do you need to know to turn your vision into reality?

17. What do you need to have done to turn your vision into reality?

18. What do you need to believe in order to turn your vision into reality?

19. What do you need to be doing 6 months / 1 year / 5 years before your vision becomes a reality?

20. If there were no constraints, what would you do? If you suspended doubt and worry, what action would you take?

21. What problems do you solve?

22. How do you help co-workers / clients / customers?

23. Who's one or two steps ahead that you can learn from?

24. If we're sitting here a year from now celebrating something huge, what would it be?

25. What matters most to you in your overall career/business?

26. What's the cost in time, money, reputation, energy, or other resources?

27. Why haven't you done this before?

28. Are we asking the right questions?

29. What are the facts in this situation?

30. What's next?

31. How do you describe success in this situation?

32. What dependencies does this project / decision / action have?

33. What do you think will happen if you say no to this request?

34. What's the cascading effect of saying yes?

35. What's the cascading effect of saying no?

36. What's more important for this (project/situation) time or money?

37. What's more important for this (project/situation) quality or quantity?
38. What's more important for this (project/situation) people or process?
39. What are all the possible ways of completing this task/project?
40. Is there an easier way?
41. What do we need more clarity about?
42. How will you experience your business relationships and conversations one year form now if you do nothing to change or improve them?
43. Have you done this before? If so, what happened?
44. What would you like this to look like in three months' time?
45. What's missing from this picture so far?
46. What did you learn from the biggest mistake you ever made?
47. What are the possible solutions to address this situation or gap?
48. What changes do you need to initiate, and how will you initiate those changes?
49. What are your plans to manage the cost of implementing changes?
50. Are you moving in a direction of your choosing? If not, what do you choose to do about it? When?
51. What do you do better than anyone else?
52. What's unique about the way you do what you do (the way you achieve results)?
53. What most strongly sets you apart from your peers?
54. What five words (adjectives) would you use to describe yourself?
55. What opportunities can you see in your situation?

56. What do you know so far about the situation?
57. What do you still need to know about the situation?
58. What resources can you call on to help?
59. How would you prioritize your options?
60. Is there a better way to measure success or progress?
61. How are you measuring success?
62. What has changed since you chose that measure of success? Is it still relevant?
63. When have you been in a similar situation?
64. What are you responsible for?
65. What have you been doing automatically, which may need reexamined?
66. What do you want from this?
67. What do you expect from this?
68. What's working?
69. What was working but is not longer?
70. What's not working?
71. What is easier now?
72. What is faster now?
73. What's possible?
74. Who's one or two steps behind that you can help?
75. What aren't you struggling with that you should be? (This is about growth - we need struggle to grow but we need to struggle with the right thing).
76. How can you avoid discussing things you've already agreed on and move onto the difficult conversations?
77. What if you didn't do it?
78. What if you stopped doing it?
79. When will you know that this approach is no longer working?
80. Why did you make this decision? Is it still true?
81. What action will make the greatest difference?

82. Are you listening to all contributors regardless of position / authority?
83. Who needs to know?
84. Who needs to be involved?
85. How will this impact others?
86. Whose opinion matters in this situation?
87. What's the problem you're trying to solve?
88. Why this problem?
89. Why solve this problem now?
90. Who's impacted by this action?
91. What is it you're not seeing?
92. Why?
93. Why not?
94. What happened?
95. Who's impacted by this decision?
96. What's the benefit?
97. What's the worst that could happen?
98. What's the best that could happen?
99. What's the most likely outcome?
100. Do you have to be at this meeting or event?
101. What do you need to do differently to use your time more effectively?
102. What do you spend too much time on that has little or no value?
103. What's not getting done?
104. What's in the way of getting this done?
105. Are your expectations realistic?
106. Is this the right time for this conversation / project / action?
107. If not now, when?
108. How do you want them to behave differently?
109. Who has recently done this task/project

successfully/unsuccessfully and how can you learn from them?

110. What should you/your team do more of?
111. What should you/your team do less of?
112. What should your/your team start doing?
113. What should you/your team stop doing?
114. What should you/your team learn how to do?
115. What should you/your team be more open to?
116. What should you/your team be firm on?
117. Where are the bottlenecks in your business/process? Where is the work piled up?
118. What resource is most at risk of running out?
119. Who on your team is overwhelmed?
120. Who is the most stressed on the team?
121. Who do you hear from the least?
122. Who do you hear from the most?
123. What's the most common question asked about this project / task / product / requirement?
124. What's the first step?
125. What's the elephant in the room for this meeting / conversation / project / decision?
126. What isn't being said that needs to be?
127. What are you experiencing right now in your business conversations that causes you concern?
128. How will developing stronger communication skills help ease your conversational concerns?
129. Who does this serve?
130. Pretend..."What if...?"
131. What's your backup plan?
132. How can you avoid sunk-cost bias?
133. Are you realistically estimating the time / cost to complete this project / task?

134. How will you know you've been successful in achieving your goal?
135. Visit the future and predict..."what would that look like next year?"
136. What's your plan and when will you begin?
137. What are potential obstacles and how will you overcome them?
138. Who's affected by this situation?
139. When you resolve this issue, what will be different?
140. What past events do you want to avoid repeating?
141. What past events are you re-writing to appear more successful?
142. What are you struggling with that you shouldn't be?
143. If you were to receive an award, what would it be for?
144. What's the business impact of this situation?

CAREER CLARITY

1. What matters most to you in this situation?
2. What's important here?
3. What's within your control?
4. What's outside your control?
5. What are your assumptions?
6. How will this impact those important to you?
7. What are your choices?
8. What would your role model do in this situation?
9. What can you learn from this situation so far?
10. Does it make you happy?
11. Is this a need or a want?
12. What can you do right now, today, to move closer to achieving your goal?
13. Where do you need to focus your energy right now?
14. What are you avoiding?
15. What unique contribution can you make?
16. What are you truly committed to?
17. What are you ready to commit to right now?

18. What is this year's guidepost?
19. How would you rate / describe your satisfaction with respect to: work? Is that what you want? If not, what do you want to be different here?
20. What 10 books will you read this year to stay relevant?
21. What has worked for you in the past in similar situations?
22. How do you want this situation to be different from prior situations?
23. What do you need to do right now?
24. What do you need to know?
25. Are you being overly negative about this?
26. Are you being overly positive about this?
27. What are you afraid of?
28. What do you want?
29. How would you rate / describe your satisfaction with respect to: finances? Is that what you want? If not, what do you want to be different here?
30. What do you want to be different next (week / quarter / year)?
31. What's your vision of your professional future in 5 / 10 / 15 years?
32. What's your vision of your lifestyle in 5 / 10 / 15 years?
33. What will it take to make your vision a reality?
34. What do you need to know to turn your vision into reality?
35. What do you need to have done to turn your vision into reality?
36. What do you need to believe in order to turn your vision into reality?
37. What do you need to be doing 6 months / 1 year / 5 years before your vision becomes a reality?

38. If there were no constraints, what would you do? If you suspended doubt and worry, what action would you take?
39. Are you drained or energized by this?
40. Are your thoughts / feelings / or actions keeping you from succeeding?
41. What is your superpower?
42. What problems do you solve?
43. How do you help co-workers / clients / customers?
44. What do you need to be thinking / doing / feeling / saying differently to make that a reality?
45. What's frustrating you right now?
46. Who's one or two steps ahead that you can learn from?
47. What are you tolerating in your professional life right now?
48. What's your top character strength?
49. What do other people experience as your top character strength?
50. What's your weakness?
51. How will you reduce the negative impact of your most prominent weakness in your work / conversations / relationships?
52. Who's your mentor? What qualities do you admire most in them?
53. What's keeping you from delivering your best work everyday?
54. What's the biggest mistake you've ever made, and why was that a good thing?
55. What's your process for deciding whether or not to take on a project?
56. If we're sitting here a year from now celebrating something huge, what would it be?

57. What relevant qualities and skills do you already have and how can you apply them to the current situation?
58. Where could you use this skill in the future?
59. What five individuals do you spend the most time with?
60. What five individuals do you want to spend more time with?
61. What matters most to you in your overall career/business?
62. What's the cost in time, money, reputation, energy, or other resources?
63. Why haven't you done this before?
64. Are we asking the right questions?
65. What are the facts in this situation?
66. Is there a way to test-drive the opportunity?
67. What's next?
68. How do you describe success in this situation?
69. What dependencies does this project / decision / action have?
70. What information do you need to make this decision?
71. When do you need to make this decision?
72. What do you think will happen if you say no to this request?
73. What's the cascading effect of saying yes?
74. What's the cascading effect of saying no?
75. Are you basing your decision on current or past information?
76. What area / skill may you be at risk of thinking you're better than you actually are?
77. What area / skill may you be at risk of thinking you're worse than you actually are?
78. Who in your professional life can you count on to be a true accountability partner?

79. What do you need from your accountability partner?
80. What can you stop doing to make room for positive change?
81. In what team role do you feel most confident?
82. What's your preferred form of communication?
83. What's more important for this (project/situation) time or money?
84. What's more important for this (project/situation) quality or quantity?
85. What's more important for this (project/situation) people or process?
86. What are all the possible ways of completing this task/project?
87. Is there an easier way?
88. What do we need more clarity about?
89. How will you experience your business relationships and conversations one year form now if you do nothing to change or improve them?
90. Who in your professional life can you count on to provide you with honest, constructive feedback?
91. What do you need your boss / manager to know in order to be successful?
92. What do you need your partner to know in order to be successful?
93. What resources do you need?
94. Why do you work?
95. What knowledge do you need?
96. What behaviors or habits do you need to change?
97. What's the best approach to making this decision?
98. Have you done this before? If so, what happened?
99. What would you like this to look like in three months' time?

100. How can a trusted advisor assist with this situation?
101. What do you want to be doing all day?
102. If you won the lottery and didn't need to work, ho would you spend your time?
103. Do you feel secure in your current earning power?
104. What's missing from this picture so far?
105. What are you doing now to shape your life tomorrow?
106. What do you really want - specifically?
107. What are the three most important elements of a life filled with joy?
108. When was the last time you lost track of time? What were you doing at the time?
109. What did you learn from the biggest mistake you ever made?
110. What do others tell you is your greatest strength?
111. What are the possible solutions to address this situation or gap?
112. What can you think, do, or feel to make this situation different?
113. What do you wish everyone would recognize in you? What strength / gift / wish?
114. Are you happy with the way things are going? if not, what are you going to do about it? When?
115. How can you make what you want achievable?
116. How will you know when you've got what you want?
117. How will things (your life, your interactions, your thoughts, your behaviors) be different once you have what you want?
118. What important choices are available to you now? ln five years' time what decision will you be glad you had now made?

119. What's the most useful thing you could do right now to take you where you want to go?

120. What changes do you need to initiate, and how will you initiate those changes?

121. What are your plans to manage the cost of implementing changes?

122. Are you moving in a direction of your choosing? If not, what do you choose to do about it? When?

123. What do you do better than anyone else?

124. What's unique about the way you do what you do (the way you achieve results)?

125. What words do people use to describe you when they introduce you to others?

126. What's the part of your job you love the most?

127. In what situations are you most naturally yourself?

128. What unique ingredient do you contribute to everything you do that without you would be missed?

129. What makes you feel most confident?

130. What do people come to you for?

131. What are you most proud of?

132. What makes you lose track of time when you do it?

133. Around whom do you feel most comfortable?

134. How would you describe your peers?

135. What do you and your peers have in common?

136. If you had a magic wand and could solve any world problem, what problem would you solve?

137. About what topic(s) can you talk endlessly?

138. What most strongly sets you apart from your peers?

139. If you had to focus the rest of your life on one thing, what would it be?

140. In what environment are you most comfortable?

141. What gets you out of bed early on a weekend to do?

142. What five words (adjectives) would you use to describe yourself?
143. What keeps you up at night?
144. Who are you becoming?
145. What opportunities can you see in your situation?
146. What do you know so far about the situation?
147. What do you still need to know about the situation?
148. What resources can you call on to help?
149. What's emerging here for you? What new connections are you making?
150. How would you prioritize your options?
151. How can your coach/mentor support you in taking the next step?
152. What unique contribution can your coach/mentor make to help you move forward?
153. What do you need from your boss / manager to be successful?
154. What do you need from your partner to be successful?
155. What are you missing in your life/work?
156. Is there a critical deadline associated with this project/goal?
157. Is there a better way to measure success or progress?
158. How are you measuring success?
159. What has changed since you chose that measure of success? Is it still relevant?

COACHING: SELF AND OTHERS

1. What are you not admitting in this situation?
2. What's important here?
3. What are your assumptions?
4. When have you been in a similar situation?
5. Are your expectations realistic?
6. Why does it matter?
7. Is that true?
8. If you viewed things from another person's point of view, what new information would that perspective give you?
9. What are your choices?
10. What can you learn from this situation so far?
11. What unique contribution can you make?
12. What are you responsible for?
13. How will this impact others?
14. What are you relying too heavily on? What have you anchored your opinion on?
15. How will this impact those important to you?

16. What matters most to you in this situation?
17. What matters most to you in this moment?
18. What do you believe about yourself in this situation?
19. Why don't you say something?
20. What is this year's guidepost?
21. If there were no constraints, what would you do? If you suspended doubt and worry, what action would you take?
22. What matters most to you in your overall career/business?
23. What are the facts in this situation?
24. What's next?
25. What changes do you need to initiate, and how will you initiate those changes?
26. What are your plans to manage the cost of implementing changes?
27. Are you moving in a direction of your choosing? If not, what do you choose to do about it? When?
28. What's your backup plan?
29. What would your role model do in this situation?
30. Does it make you happy?
31. What are you truly committed to?
32. What are you ready to commit to right now?
33. How would you rate / describe your satisfaction with respect to: work? Is that what you want? If not, what do you want to be different here?
34. What are you afraid of?
35. What do you want?
36. How would you rate / describe your satisfaction with respect to: finances? Is that what you want? If not, what do you want to be different here?

37. What relevant qualities and skills do you already have and how can you apply them to the current situation?

38. What area / skill may you be at risk of thinking you're better than you actually are?

39. What area / skill may you be at risk of thinking you're worse than you actually are?

40. What can you stop doing to make room for positive change?

41. What do you really want - specifically?

42. Are you happy with the way things are going? if not, what are you going to do about it? When?

43. How can you make what you want achievable?

44. How will you know when you've got what you want?

45. How will things (your life, your interactions, your thoughts, your behaviors) be different once you have what you want?

46. What important choices are available to you now? In five years' time what decision will you be glad you had now made?

47. What's the most useful thing you could do right now to take you where you want to go?

48. Who are you becoming?

49. What would you have changed about the experience?

50. Does it matter?

51. Is it helping?

52. What is still challenging?

53. what's really happening?

54. What type of things can you do to close the gap? Reduce the difference?

55. What 10 books have you read that had significant impact for you personally or professionally?

56. What's it going to take to put you in the center of your own life?

57. How would you rate / describe your satisfaction with respect to: family? Is that what you want? If not, what do you want to be different here?

58. How would you rate / describe your satisfaction with respect to: friends/social? Is that what you want? If not, what do you want to be different here?

59. How would you rate / describe your satisfaction with respect to: health? Is that what you want? If not, what do you want to be different here?

60. How would you rate / describe your satisfaction with respect to: spirituality? Is that what you want? If not, what do you want to be different here?

61. What things do you like or dislike in each area of your life/business?

62. What is really important to you - rather than merely urgent? What is your underlying purpose here?

63. What about yourself do you loath?

64. Is there anything that you are not noticing that you need to pay attention to? If you were an objective observer of yourself, what would you now say?

65. How can you listen more to your inner wisdom?

66. What do you believe that limits you? What assumptions have you been making that are no longer valid?

67. What are you holding onto (ideas/things/beliefs/habits) that no longer serve you?

68. What do you regret? How can you avoid that specific regret in the future?

69. What makes you uncomfortable? Is there something to learn from that?

70. If you could do (whatever you've regretted) over, what would be different?
71. And then what? (What happens next in this scenario?)
72. Why don't you do something?
73. What will you do to transform the 50,000 thoughts you have each day into mostly positive instead of the normal mostly negative?
74. What good will you do today?
75. What good have you done today?
76. By when?
77. What's stopping you?
78. What about this excites you?
79. What's this costing you?
80. What are you learning from this?
81. What else?
82. Who else?
83. Like what?
84. How else?
85. How could you?
86. What's it like?
87. What are you discovering?
88. What do you mean?
89. Where will that get you?
90. What would that give you?
91. What's new about this?
92. What will change?
93. What are you resisting?
94. What will be different now?
95. What's within your power to change?
96. What about yourself do you love?
97. What do you need to acknowledge yourself for? What deserves celebration?

98. Are your habitual behaviors productive in terms of what you now want?

99. Are you directing your thinking in a useful direction? What will be the most productive direction for your thinking?

100. What would it take for you to be your own strongest ally? How can you get out of your own way?

101. What stands out?

102. What will you do next?

103. How else could you describe your behavior in this situation?

104. Does the problem really lie in the action or in the way you feel about the action?

105. When might this scenario be appropriate?

106. What we think about today will create who we are tomorrow. Are you drawing in success? Or are you drawing in defeat?

COLLABORATING

1. What are you not admitting in this situation?
2. Why does it matter?
3. What's important here?
4. What unique contribution can you make?
5. What's your point?
6. What do you want from this?
7. What do you expect from this?
8. Are your expectations realistic?
9. Whose opinion matters in this situation?
10. What's the cost in time, money, reputation, energy, or other resources?
11. Is that true?
12. Who needs to know?
13. Who needs to be involved?
14. How will this impact others?
15. What are your assumptions?
16. What can you learn from this situation so far?
17. What are they thinking, feeling, and wanting?

18. What are you responsible for?
19. What are your choices?
20. When have you been in a similar situation?
21. What are you having a hard time believing because of who's sharing the information?
22. How can you avoid discussing things you've already agree on and move onto the difficult conversations?
23. If you viewed things from another person's point of view, what new information would that perspective give you?
24. What impact has this meant for others at work?
25. What are you relying too heavily on? What have you anchored your opinion on?
26. What have you been doing automatically, which may need reexamined?
27. Who in your professional life can you count on to provide you with honest, constructive feedback?
28. Who in your professional life can you count on to be a true accountability partner?
29. What do you need from your accountability partner?
30. Who plays the supporting role to you as the hero? Who is your biggest fan?
31. What evidence would you give to someone who doubted your interpretation?
32. Are you judging based on your own values or theirs?
33. Who's impacted by this action?

COMMUNICATING

1. What are you not admitting in this situation?
2. Who did you make a genuine connection with today?
3. What's important here?
4. What are your assumptions?
5. How will this impact those important to you?
6. How will you experience your business relationships and conversations one year form now if you do nothing to change or improve them?
7. When have you been in a similar situation?
8. What have you been doing automatically, which may need reexamined?
9. What do you want from this?
10. What do you expect from this?
11. Who needs to know?
12. Who needs to be involved?
13. Whose opinion matters in this situation?
14. Are your expectations realistic?

15. Is this the right time for this conversation / project / action?
16. What are you experiencing right now in your business conversations that causes you concern?
17. How will developing stronger communication skills help ease your conversational concerns?
18. What matters most to you in this situation?
19. What five individuals do you spend the most time with?
20. What five individuals do you want to spend more time with?
21. What's your preferred form of communication?
22. What matters most to you in this moment?
23. Why does it matter?
24. Is that true?
25. What are you not telling your boss / partner that they need to know?
26. What do you believe about yourself in this situation?
27. What are you having a hard time believing because of who's sharing the information?
28. What do you think they should know without me telling them? Is that reasonable?
29. How is sharing this information / opinion about someone else (who is not present) going to help them?
30. If you viewed things from another person's point of view, what new information would that perspective give you?
31. Why don't you say something?
32. What is the most difficult conversation you've had in your professional life?
33. What do you wish you had said in that difficult conversation?
34. What had real meaning for you from what you've heard?

35. What surprised you from what you've heard?
36. What challenged you from what you've heard?
37. How much time and energy will you devote to improving your communication skills?
38. What evidence would you give to someone who doubted your interpretation?
39. Can you put that anther way?
40. What's your point?
41. What are they thinking, feeling, and wanting?
42. Is what I'm about to say helping to achieve our/my goal? Does it add value?

CONFIDENCE

1. What are you not admitting in this situation?
2. Is that true?
3. What's important here?
4. What matters most to you in this moment?
5. Does it make you happy?
6. Is it helping?
7. What good have you done today?
8. Is this a need or a want?
9. What are you afraid of?
10. What's it going to take to put you in the center of your own life?
11. What will you do to transform the 50,000 thoughts you have each day into mostly positive instead of the normal mostly negative?
12. What we think about today will create who we are tomorrow. Are you drawing in success? Or are you drawing in defeat?
13. What's the benefit?

14. Why does it matter?
15. What are your choices?
16. What are your assumptions?
17. Are your expectations realistic?
18. What do you want from this?
19. What do you expect from this?
20. What unique contribution can you make?
21. What do you do better than anyone else?
22. What's unique about the way you do what you do (the way you achieve results)?
23. What five words (adjectives) would you use to describe yourself?
24. If you were to receive an award, what would it be for?
25. What do others tell you is your greatest strength?
26. What unique ingredient do you contribute to everything you do that without you would be missed?
27. What do people come to you for?
28. What are you most proud of?
29. About what topic(s) can you talk endlessly?
30. What do you like best about yourself?
31. What's the most unique/quirkiest think about you?
32. What are the three most important elements of a life filled with joy?
33. What's the part of your job you love the most?
34. In what situations are you most naturally yourself?
35. What makes you feel most confident?
36. What makes you lose track of time when you do it?
37. What gets you out of bed early on a weekend to do?
38. What's your biggest hope or dream?
39. What quality in others do you admire the most?
40. What was the best decision you ever made? Why?
41. What are you truly committed to?

42. How can you listen more to your inner wisdom?
43. What makes you uncomfortable? Is there something to learn from that?
44. What's within your control?
45. What's outside your control?
46. What can you do right now, today, to move closer to achieving your goal?
47. What are you avoiding?
48. When have you been in a similar situation?
49. What do you believe about yourself in this situation?
50. Why don't you say something?
51. What do you want?
52. Who are you becoming?
53. Does it matter?
54. What about yourself do you love?
55. Who did you make a genuine connection with today?
56. If we're sitting here a year from now celebrating something huge, what would it be?
57. Are you being overly negative about this?
58. What problems do you solve?
59. How do you help co-workers / clients / customers?
60. Who's one or two steps ahead that you can learn from?
61. How do you describe success in this situation?
62. What's working?
63. What's possible?
64. What's the worst that could happen?
65. What's the best that could happen?
66. What's the most likely outcome?
67. What has worked for you in the past in similar situations?
68. How do you want this situation to be different from prior situations?

69. Are your thoughts / feelings / or actions keeping you from succeeding?
70. What is your superpower?
71. What's your top character strength?
72. What information do you need to make this decision?
73. What can you think, do, or feel to make this situation different?
74. What's emerging here for you? What new connections are you making?
75. How are these thoughts impacting your decision making, behavior, focus, productivity, or happiness?
76. What are you feeling right now?
77. Why do you feel this way?
78. What triggered this feeling?
79. What recurring thoughts are you having?
80. What do you need to be different in order to move forward on this matter?
81. Do you trust yourself?
82. Are these thoughts / feelings / actions related to this situation or something else entirely?

CONSULTING

1. What's important here?
2. What are your choices?
3. What are you responsible for?
4. What are your assumptions?
5. Are your expectations realistic?
6. What can you learn from this situation so far?
7. How will this impact others?
8. What matters most to you in this situation?
9. What have you been doing automatically, which may need reexamined?
10. What do you want from this?
11. What do you expect from this?
12. Who needs to know?
13. Who needs to be involved?
14. Whose opinion matters in this situation?
15. What's the cost in time, money, reputation, energy, or other resources?

16. How can you avoid discussing things you've already agreed on and move onto the difficult conversations?
17. Are we asking the right questions?
18. When will you know that this approach is no longer working?
19. Why did you make this decision? Is it still true?
20. Are you listening to all contributors regardless of position / authority?
21. What's the problem you're trying to solve?
22. Why this problem?
23. Why solve this problem now?
24. What happened?
25. How do you want them to behave differently?
26. What should you/your team do more of?
27. What should you/your team do less of?
28. What should your/your team start doing?
29. What should you/your team stop doing?
30. What should you/your team learn how to do?
31. What should you/your team be more open to?
32. What should you/your team be firm on?

DECISION MAKING

1. How can you avoid discussing things you've already agreed on and move onto the difficult conversations?
2. Does it matter?
3. Why does it matter?
4. What matters most to you in this situation?
5. What's important here?
6. What are you responsible for?
7. What's the cost in time, money, reputation, energy, or other resources?
8. What if you didn't do it?
9. What dependencies does this project / decision / action have?
10. Why haven't you done this before?
11. What if you stopped doing it?
12. When will you know that this approach is no longer working?
13. Why did you make this decision? Is it still true?
14. What matters most to you in this moment?

15. What's within your control?
16. What's outside your control?
17. What action will make the greatest difference?
18. Are you listening to all contributors regardless of position / authority?
19. Who's impacted by this decision?
20. Are we asking the right questions?
21. What are your assumptions?
22. What are the facts in this situation?
23. What's the benefit?
24. Who needs to know?
25. Who needs to be involved?
26. How will this impact those important to you?
27. What are your choices?
28. How will this impact others?
29. Whose opinion matters in this situation?
30. What's the problem you're trying to solve?
31. Why this problem?
32. Why solve this problem now?
33. What are you having a hard time believing because of who's sharing the information?
34. What are you relying too heavily on? What have you anchored your opinion on?
35. Does it make you happy?
36. Is this a need or a want?
37. How are these thoughts impacting your decision-making, behavior, focus, productivity, or happiness?
38. What would your role model do in this situation?
39. What's the worst that could happen?
40. What's the best that could happen?
41. What's the most likely outcome?
42. What information do you need to make this decision?

43. When do you need to make this decision?
44. What do you think will happen if you say no to this request?
45. What's the cascading effect of saying yes?
46. What's the cascading effect of saying no?
47. Do you trust yourself?
48. When should you stop asking others for input on decisions?
49. What decisions have you made similar to this one? How can you learn from that to help you decide now?
50. In the worst-case scenario, what happens down the road?
51. Are you basing your decision on current or past information?
52. Have you considered the most relevant information or are you only using what is easily available?
53. When considering this opportunity, do you feel expansive (feeling of something big, positive, exciting) or contractive (closed, small, limited)?
54. How exactly would you deal with the worst-case scenario? What are the exact steps you would take to get back from the worst-case scenario?
55. What are the possible payoffs for saying yes to this opportunity? Be specific.
56. Is there a way to test-drive the opportunity?

DELEGATING

1. What do you think they should know without me telling them? Is that reasonable?
2. How do you want them to behave differently?
3. Do you have to be at this meeting or event?
4. How much time should you spend planning versus doing in this situation?
5. What action will make the greatest difference?
6. What do you need them to know, in order to feel comfortable delegating this task to this person?
7. What would you like to take off your 'plate' / 'responsibility list'?
8. What needs to happen in order for you to take that item off your plate / list?
9. What do you need to do differently to use your time more effectively?
10. What one thing can you remove from you to-do list - forever?

11. Who in your professional life can you count on to be a true accountability partner?
12. What do you need from your accountability partner?
13. What can you stop doing to make room for positive change?

DIFFICULT CONVERSATIONS

1. How do you think the other person views the situation?
2. What are you not telling your boss / partner that they need to know?
3. Are you judging based on your own values or theirs?
4. What's the elephant in the room for this meeting / conversation / project / decision?
5. What isn't being said that needs to be?
6. Why don't you say something?
7. Why don't you do something?
8. What is the most difficult conversation you've had in your professional life?
9. What do you wish you had said in that difficult conversation?
10. How is sharing this information / opinion about someone else (who is not present) going to help them?
11. What had real meaning for you from what you've heard?
12. What surprised you from what you've heard?
13. What challenged you from what you've heard?

14. What do we need more clarity about?
15. What are you experiencing right now in your business conversations that causes you concern?
16. How will developing stronger communication skills help ease your conversational concerns?
17. How will you experience your business relationships and conversations one year form now if you do nothing to change or improve them?
18. How much time and energy will you devote to improving your communication skills?
19. Who in your professional life can you count on to provide you with honest, constructive feedback?
20. What do you need your boss / manager to know in order to be successful?
21. What do you need your partner to know in order to be successful?
22. What evidence would you give to someone who doubted your interpretation?

FINANCE

1. How would you rate / describe your satisfaction with respect to: finances? Is that what you want? If not, what do you want to be different here?
2. What type of things can you do to close the gap? Reduce the difference?
3. What's the benefit?
4. What resources do you need?
5. Are your expectations realistic?
6. What's the worst that could happen?
7. What's the best that could happen?
8. What's the most likely outcome?
9. Is this a need or a want?
10. What matters most to you in this situation?
11. What's the cost in time, money, reputation, energy, or other resources?
12. How will this impact others?
13. What are the facts in this situation?
14. What are you responsible for?

15. What are your choices?
16. What information do you need to make this decision?
17. How can you avoid sunk cost bias?
18. Are you realistically estimating the time / cost to complete this project / task?
19. What do you want to be different next (week / quarter / year)?
20. What resource is most at risk of running out?
21. What's more important for this (project/situation) time or money?
22. If you won the lottery and didn't need to work, ho would you spend your time?
23. Are you judging based on your own values or theirs?
24. How much money do you earn?
25. How much money do you keep?
26. How much money do you save?
27. Do you feel secure in your current earning power?
28. Can you survive an unexpected financial burden of $500? $5,000? $50,000?
29. Do you know where every penny of your earned money goes each month?
30. Do you have a financial plan for this quarter / year?
31. How do you track your earnings and spending?
32. What are your detailed expected expenses for the coming 18 months?
33. What can you put in place to adhere to your financial plan?
34. Where in your business can you use a creative solution to avoid increasing your debt?

GOALS AND FOCUSING

1. What's important here?
2. If you viewed things from another person's point of view, what new information would that perspective give you?
3. What are your choices?
4. What unique contribution can you make?
5. What are you responsible for?
6. What matters most to you in this moment?
7. What is this year's guidepost?
8. If there were no constraints, what would you do? If you suspended doubt and worry, what action would you take?
9. What matters most to you in your overall career/business?
10. What's next?
11. What changes do you need to initiate, and how will you initiate those changes?

12. What are your plans to manage the cost of implementing changes?
13. Are you moving in a direction of your choosing? If not, what do you choose to do about it? When?
14. What are you truly committed to?
15. What are you ready to commit to right now?
16. How would you rate / describe your satisfaction with respect to: work? Is that what you want? If not, what do you want to be different here?
17. How would you rate / describe your satisfaction with respect to: finances? Is that what you want? If not, what do you want to be different here?
18. What relevant qualities and skills do you already have and how can you apply them to the current situation?
19. What do you really want - specifically?
20. Are you happy with the way things are going? if not, what are you going to do about it? When?
21. How can you make what you want achievable?
22. How will you know when you've got what you want?
23. How will things (your life, your interactions, your thoughts, your behaviors) be different once you have what you want?
24. What important choices are available to you now? In five years' time what decision will you be glad you had now made?
25. What's the most useful thing you could do right now to take you where you want to go?
26. Is it helping?
27. What type of things can you do to close the gap? Reduce the difference?
28. How would you rate / describe your satisfaction with

respect to: family? Is that what you want? If not, what do you want to be different here?

29. How would you rate / describe your satisfaction with respect to: friends/social? Is that what you want? If not, what do you want to be different here?

30. How would you rate / describe your satisfaction with respect to: health? Is that what you want? If not, what do you want to be different here?

31. How would you rate / describe your satisfaction with respect to: spirituality? Is that what you want? If not, what do you want to be different here?

32. What things do you like or dislike in each area of your life/business?

33. What is really important to you - rather than merely urgent? What is your underlying purpose here?

34. Is there anything that you are not noticing that you need to pay attention to? If you were an objective observer of yourself, what would you now say?

35. How can you listen more to your inner wisdom?

36. What do you believe that limits you? What assumptions have you been making that are no longer valid?

37. What do you regret? How can you avoid that specific regret in the future?

38. What makes you uncomfortable? Is there something to learn from that?

39. If you could do (whatever you've regretted) over, what would be different?

40. What good will you do today?

41. What good have you done today?

42. What do you need to acknowledge yourself for? What deserves celebration?

43. Are your habitual behaviors productive in terms of what you now want?

44. Are you directing your thinking in a useful direction? What will be the most productive direction for your thinking?

45. What would it take for you to be your own strongest ally? How can you get out of your own way?

46. Is what I'm about to say helping to achieve our/my goal? Does it add value?

47. Where do you need to focus your energy right now?

48. If not now, when?

49. What's the first step?

50. What's within your control?

51. What's outside your control?

52. Is this a need or a want?

53. What can you do right now, today, to move closer to achieving your goal?

54. What are you avoiding?

55. What would help sustain positive momentum?

56. What are the possible payoffs for saying yes to this opportunity? Be specific.

57. What does 'done' look like?

58. What can you do today to focus more on what's important and essential?

59. Who needs your undivided attention today?

60. What project / task needs your undivided attention today?

61. What distracts you from your most important work?

62. What energy are you putting in to achieving your goals?

63. Where are you along your plan?

GOING FREELANCE

1. How will this impact those important to you?
2. What's the benefit?
3. What resources do you need?
4. Are your expectations realistic?
5. What's the worst that could happen?
6. What's the best that could happen?
7. What's the most likely outcome?
8. What matters most to you in this situation?
9. What's the cost in time, money, reputation, energy, or other resources?
10. How will this impact others?
11. What are you responsible for?
12. What are your choices?
13. What information do you need to make this decision?
14. How can you avoid sunk cost bias?
15. Are you realistically estimating the time / cost to complete this project / task?
16. How much money do you earn?

17. What are your detailed expected expenses for the coming 18 months?
18. What can you put in place to adhere to your financial plan?
19. Where in your business can you use a creative solution to avoid increasing your debt?
20. What is this year's guidepost?
21. Does it make you happy?
22. How do you describe success in this situation?
23. What unique contribution can you make?
24. How would you rate / describe your satisfaction with respect to: work? Is that what you want? If not, what do you want to be different here?
25. Why do you work?
26. Who needs to know?
27. Who needs to be involved?
28. By when?
29. What's stopping you?
30. What about this excites you?
31. What's this costing you?
32. What's your backup plan?
33. Who's impacted by this decision?
34. Who's impacted by this action?
35. How will you know you've been successful in achieving your goal?
36. What's the first step?
37. What knowledge do you need?
38. What behaviors or habits do you need to change?
39. What structure and support do you need?
40. If not now, when?
41. What 10 books will you read this year to stay relevant?
42. What do you want from this?

43. What do you expect from this?
44. What if you didn't do it?
45. What matters most to you in your overall career/business?
46. Whose opinion matters in this situation?
47. What are your assumptions?
48. What's within your control?
49. What's outside your control?
50. When have you been in a similar situation?
51. What has worked for you in the past in similar situations?
52. How do you want this situation to be different from prior situations?
53. What do you need to do right now?
54. What do you need to know?
55. Is this the right time for this conversation / project / action?
56. When do you need to make this decision?
57. Is the obstacle real or imagined?
58. What's the best approach to making this decision?
59. What do you think will happen if you say no to this request?
60. What's the cascading effect of saying yes?
61. What's the cascading effect of saying no?
62. What dependencies does this project / decision / action have?
63. Why haven't you done this before?
64. Have you done this before? If so, what happened?
65. Are you being overly negative about this?
66. Are you being overly positive about this?
67. What can you do right now, today, to move closer to achieving your goal?

68. Visit the future and predict..."what would that look like next year?"
69. Approach from different places..."What would your heart say? What about your head/brain/ younger self / older self?"
70. What will change?
71. What are you resisting?
72. What would you like this to look like in three months' time?
73. How can a trusted advisor assist with this situation?
74. What's your plan and when will you begin?
75. What are potential obstacles and how will you overcome them?
76. What feedback will help you along the way?
77. How much time should you spend planning versus doing in this situation?
78. Do you trust yourself?
79. Why do you want to go out on your own?
80. What do you want to be doing all day?
81. When should you stop asking others for input on decisions?
82. What decisions have you made similar to this one? How can you learn from that to help you decide now?

HABITS AND BEHAVIORS

1. What are you not admitting in this situation?
2. Is that true?
3. What's important here?
4. What matters most to you in this moment?
5. What's next?
6. How will this impact those important to you?
7. Does it make you happy?
8. What matters most to you in this situation?
9. What have you been doing automatically, which may need reexamined?
10. What's the cost in time, money, reputation, energy, or other resources?
11. When will you know that this approach is no longer working?
12. What is this year's guidepost?
13. Is it helping?
14. What good will you do today?
15. What good have you done today?

16. Where do you need to focus your energy right now?

17. Is this a need or a want?

18. What would help sustain positive momentum?

19. What are you afraid of?

20. What would you have changed about the experience?

21. What's it going to take to put you in the center of your own life?

22. Why don't you do something?

23. What will you do to transform the 50,000 thoughts you have each day into mostly positive instead of the normal mostly negative?

24. How else could you describe your behavior in this situation?

25. When might this scenario be appropriate?

26. What we think about today will create who we are tomorrow. Are you drawing in success? Or are you drawing in defeat?

27. What five individuals do you spend the most time with?

28. What five individuals do you want to spend more time with?

29. What if you didn't do it?

30. What if you stopped doing it?

31. What's the benefit?

32. What do you need to do differently to use your time more effectively?

33. Who does this serve?

34. What is the better version of you?

35. What's keeping you busy?

36. What are you REALLY hungry for?

LISTENING

1. What are you not admitting in this situation?
2. Is that true?
3. What's important here?
4. What matters most to you in this moment?
5. What's next?
6. Why does it matter?
7. How will this impact those important to you?
8. Does it make you happy?
9. What's your point?
10. What are your concerns and worries about the situation?

PERSONAL GROWTH

1. What matters most to you in this situation?
2. What's important here?
3. What matters most to you in this moment?
4. What's within your control?
5. What's outside your control?
6. What are your assumptions?
7. How will this impact those important to you?
8. What are your choices?
9. What would your role model do in this situation?
10. When have you been in a similar situation?
11. What can you learn from this situation so far?
12. What are your perceptions on why this situation has occurred?
13. What can we do to rectify the situation?
14. What would you have changed about the experience?
15. Does it matter?
16. Why does it matter?
17. What are you responsible for?

18. Does it make you happy?
19. Is this a need or a want?
20. How are these thoughts impacting your decision-making, behavior, focus, productivity, or happiness?
21. What are you not admitting in this situation?
22. What have you been doing automatically, which may need reexamined?
23. What do you want from this?
24. What do you expect from this?
25. Is that true?
26. What can you do right now, today, to move closer to achieving your goal?
27. Where do you need to focus your energy right now?
28. What are you avoiding?
29. What would help sustain positive momentum?
30. What learning format best suits your style or preference?
31. What unique contribution can you make?
32. What are you truly committed to?
33. What are you ready to commit to right now?
34. Is it helping?
35. What's working?
36. What was working but is not longer?
37. What's not working?
38. What is easier now?
39. What is faster now?
40. What is still challenging?
41. What are you not telling your boss / partner that they need to know?
42. what's really happening?
43. What do you believe about yourself in this situation?
44. What is this year's guidepost?

45. How would you rate / describe your satisfaction with respect to: work? Is that what you want? If not, what do you want to be different here?
46. What 10 books will you read this year to stay relevant?
47. What has worked for you in the past in similar situations?
48. How do you want this situation to be different from prior situations?
49. What do you need to do right now?
50. What do you need to know?
51. Are you being overly negative about this?
52. Are you being overly positive about this?
53. What are you afraid of?
54. What do you want?
55. What type of things can you do to close the gap? Reduce the difference?
56. How would you rate / describe your satisfaction with respect to: finances? Is that what you want? If not, what do you want to be different here?
57. What do you want to be different next (week / quarter / year)?
58. What is the better version of you?
59. What's it going to take to put you in the center of your own life?
60. What's your vision of your professional future in 5 / 10 / 15 years?
61. What's your vision of your lifestyle in 5 / 10 / 15 years?
62. What will it take to make your vision a reality?
63. What do you need to know to turn your vision into reality?
64. What do you need to have done to turn your vision into reality?

65. What do you need to believe in order to turn your vision into reality?
66. What do you need to be doing 6 months / 1 year / 5 years before your vision becomes a reality?
67. How would you rate / describe your satisfaction with respect to: family? Is that what you want? If not, what do you want to be different here?
68. How would you rate / describe your satisfaction with respect to: friends/social? Is that what you want? If not, what do you want to be different here?
69. How would you rate / describe your satisfaction with respect to: health? Is that what you want? If not, what do you want to be different here?
70. How would you rate / describe your satisfaction with respect to: spirituality? Is that what you want? If not, what do you want to be different here?
71. What things do you like or dislike in each area of your life/business?
72. What is really important to you - rather than merely urgent? What is your underlying purpose here?
73. If there were no constraints, what would you do? If you suspended doubt and worry, what action would you take?
74. Are you drained or energized by this?
75. What's possible?
76. What are you feeling right now?
77. Why do you feel this way?
78. What triggered this feeling?
79. What biases are you depending on?
80. What recurring thoughts are you having?
81. Are your thoughts / feelings / or actions keeping you from succeeding?

82. Who are you avoiding and why?
83. What is your superpower?
84. What problems do you solve?
85. How do you help co-workers / clients / customers?
86. What do you need to be different in order to move forward on this matter?
87. What do you need to be thinking / doing / feeling / saying differently to make that a reality?
88. What's frustrating you right now?
89. Who's one or two steps ahead that you can learn from?
90. Who's one or two steps behind that you can help?
91. What are you tolerating in your professional life right now?
92. What are you tolerating in your personal life right now?
93. What's your top character strength?
94. What do other people experience as your top character strength?
95. What's your weakness?
96. How will you reduce the negative impact of your most prominent weakness in your work / conversations / relationships?
97. What about yourself do you loath?
98. Who's your mentor? What qualities do you admire most in them?
99. What's keeping you from delivering your best work everyday?
100. What aren't you struggling with that you should be? (This is about growth - we need struggle to grow but we need to struggle with the right thing).
101. What's the biggest mistake you've ever made, and why was that a good thing?
102. What's the best creative advice you've ever been given?

103. What's your worst habit?

104. What's your process for deciding whether or not to take on a project?

105. If you could have one do-over, what would it be?

106. What's a habit you're trying to adopt right now?

107. If we're sitting here a year from now celebrating something huge, what would it be?

108. Is there anything that you are not noticing that you need to pay attention to? If you were an objective observer of yourself, what would you now say?

109. How can you listen more to your inner wisdom?

110. What relevant qualities and skills do you already have and how can you apply them to the current situation?

111. What do you believe that limits you? What assumptions have you been making that are no longer valid?

112. Where could you use this skill in the future?

113. What impact has this had for you?

114. What impact has this meant for others at work?

115. What five individuals do you spend the most time with?

116. What five individuals do you want to spend more time with?

117. What are you holding onto (ideas/things/beliefs/habits) that no longer serve you?

118. What do you regret? How can you avoid that specific regret in the future?

119. What makes you uncomfortable? Is there something to learn from that?

120. If you could do (whatever you've regretted) over, what would be different?

121. Who did you make a genuine connection with today?

122. What matters most to you in your overall career/business?

PROBLEM SOLVING

1. How can you avoid discussing things you've already agreed on and move onto the difficult conversations?
2. What matters most to you in this situation?
3. What's important here?
4. What's the cost in time, money, reputation, energy, or other resources?
5. What if you didn't do it?
6. Why haven't you done this before?
7. What if you stopped doing it?
8. When will you know that this approach is no longer working?
9. Why did you make this decision? Is it still true?
10. What matters most to you in this moment?
11. What's within your control?
12. What's outside your control?
13. What action will make the greatest difference?
14. Are you listening to all contributors regardless of position / authority?

15. Are we asking the right questions?
16. What are your assumptions?
17. What are the facts in this situation?
18. Who needs to know?
19. Who needs to be involved?
20. How will this impact those important to you?
21. What are your choices?
22. How will this impact others?
23. Whose opinion matters in this situation?
24. What's the problem you're trying to solve?
25. Why this problem?
26. Why solve this problem now?
27. What are you relying too heavily on? What have you anchored your opinion on?
28. What would your role model do in this situation?
29. Have you considered the most relevant information or are you only using what is easily available?
30. Is there a way to test-drive the opportunity?
31. What's next?
32. How do you describe success in this situation?
33. Who's impacted by this action?
34. What is it you're not seeing?
35. Why?
36. Why not?
37. When have you been in a similar situation?
38. What can you learn from this situation so far?
39. What happened?
40. And then what? (What happens next in this scenario?)
41. What are your perceptions on why this situation has occurred?
42. What can we do to rectify the situation?

43. What would you have changed about the experience?
44. What would you do if your job depended on the resolution of this problem?

PROCESSES

1. Is it helping?
2. If you viewed things from another person's point of view, what new information would that perspective give you?
3. Why?
4. Why not?
5. What's working?
6. What was working but is not longer?
7. What's not working?
8. What is easier now?
9. What is faster now?
10. What is still challenging?
11. What have you been doing automatically, which may need reexamined?
12. What's the first step?
13. What's more important for this (project/situation) time or money?
14. What do you think the next step could be?

15. What's not getting done?
16. What's in the way of getting this done?
17. What do you spend too much time on that has little or no value?
18. Where are the bottlenecks in your business/process? Where is the work piled up?
19. What's the most common question asked about this project/task/product/requirement?
20. Who has recently done this task/project successfully/unsuccessfully and how can you learn from them?
21. What's more important for this (project/situation) quality or quantity?
22. What's more important for this (project/situation) people or process?
23. What action will make the greatest difference?
24. What can you do today to focus more on what's important and essential?
25. Is there an easier way?

PRODUCTIVITY

1. What are you not admitting in this situation?
2. What do you think they should know without me telling them? Is that reasonable?
3. Do you have to be at this meeting or event?
4. How much time should you spend planning versus doing in this situation?
5. What do you need them to know, in order to feel comfortable delegating this task to this person?
6. What would you like to take off your 'plate' / 'responsibility list'?
7. What needs to happen in order for you to take that item off your plate / list?
8. What do you need to do differently to use your time more effectively?
9. What one thing can you remove from you to-do list - forever?
10. What have you been doing automatically, which may need reexamined?

11. How can you avoid discussing things you've already agreed on and move onto the difficult conversations?

12. What do you spend too much time on that has little or no value?

13. What area / skill may you be at risk of thinking you're better than you actually are?

14. What area / skill may you be at risk of thinking you're worse than you actually are?

15. What's not getting done?

16. What's in the way of getting this done?

17. Does it matter?

18. Why does it matter?

19. What's next?

20. What matters most to you in this situation?

21. What's important here?

22. What are you responsible for?

23. What do you want from this?

24. What do you expect from this?

25. Are your expectations realistic?

26. What's the cost in time, money, reputation, energy, or other resources?

27. How do you describe success in this situation?

28. What if you didn't do it?

29. Is this the right time for this conversation / project / action?

30. What dependencies does this project / decision / action have?

31. Why haven't you done this before?

32. What if you stopped doing it?

33. What does 'done' look like?

34. When will you know that this approach is no longer working?

35. Why did you make this decision? Is it still true?
36. What can you do today to focus more on what's important and essential?
37. Why don't you do something?
38. Is that true?
39. What matters most to you in this moment?
40. What will you do to transform the 50,000 thoughts you have each day into mostly positive instead of the normal mostly negative?
41. What's within your control?
42. What's outside your control?
43. What can you do right now, today, to move closer to achieving your goal?
44. Where do you need to focus your energy right now?
45. What are you avoiding?
46. What would help sustain positive momentum?
47. What learning format best suits your style or preference?
48. If not now, when?
49. Is the obstacle real or imagined?
50. Who needs your undivided attention today?
51. What project / task needs your undivided attention today?
52. What distracts you from your most important work?
53. What's keeping you busy?
54. What good will you do today?
55. What good have you done today?
56. What energy are you putting in to achieving your goals?

PROJECTS

1. Why?
2. Why not?
3. What have you been doing automatically, which may need reexamined?
4. What's more important for this (project/situation) time or money?
5. What's not getting done?
6. What's in the way of getting this done?
7. Who has recently done this task/project successfully/unsuccessfully and how can you learn from them?
8. What's more important for this (project/situation) quality or quantity?
9. What's more important for this (project/situation) people or process?
10. Does it matter?
11. Why does it matter?
12. What's next?

13. Are we asking the right questions?
14. What matters most to you in this situation?
15. What are your assumptions?
16. What's important here?
17. What are the facts in this situation?
18. Are you listening to all contributors regardless of position / authority?
19. What's the benefit?
20. Who needs to know?
21. Who needs to be involved?
22. How will this impact those important to you?
23. What are you responsible for?
24. What are your choices?
25. What do you want from this?
26. What do you expect from this?
27. When have you been in a similar situation?
28. What can you learn from this situation so far?
29. Are your expectations realistic?
30. What's the cost in time, money, reputation, energy, or other resources?
31. How will this impact others?
32. How do you describe success in this situation?
33. What if you didn't do it?
34. Whose opinion matters in this situation?
35. Is this the right time for this conversation / project / action?
36. What dependencies does this project / decision / action have?
37. Why haven't you done this before?
38. How much time should you spend planning versus doing in this situation?
39. What if you stopped doing it?

40. What's the problem you're trying to solve?
41. Why this problem?
42. Why solve this problem now?
43. What does 'done' look like?
44. When will you know that this approach is no longer working?
45. Why did you make this decision? Is it still true?
46. How can you avoid discussing things you've already agreed on and move onto the difficult conversations?
47. What are all the possible ways of completing this task/project?
48. What should you/your team do more of?
49. What should you/your team do less of?
50. What should your/your team start doing?
51. What should you/your team stop doing?
52. What should you/your team learn how to do?
53. What should you/your team be more open to?
54. What should you/your team be firm on?
55. In what team role do you feel most confident?
56. What's the most common question asked about this project/task/product/requirement?

REPUTATION AND BRAND

1. What unique contribution can you make?
2. What do you do better than anyone else?
3. What's unique about the way you do what you do (the way you achieve results)?
4. What most strongly sets you apart from your peers?
5. What five words (adjectives) would you use to describe yourself?
6. If you were to receive an award, what would it be for?
7. In what team role do you feel most confident?
8. What do others tell you is your greatest strength?
9. What words do people use to describe you when they introduce you to others?
10. What unique ingredient do you contribute to everything you do that without you would be missed?
11. What do people come to you for?
12. What are you most proud of?
13. Around whom do you feel most comfortable?
14. About what topic(s) can you talk endlessly?

15. In what environment are you most comfortable?
16. How is your public persona different from the real you?
17. In what circumstances are you most honest?
18. What do you like best about yourself?
19. What's the most unique/quirkiest think about you?
20. What's your favorite thing to do in your free time?

SHIFTING PERSPECTIVE

1. What are you not admitting in this situation?
2. Does it matter?
3. Why does it matter?
4. Is it helping?
5. Is that true?
6. Who does this serve?
7. What's next?
8. What happened?
9. Are we asking the right questions?
10. Can you put that anther way?
11. What matters most to you in this situation?
12. What are your assumptions?
13. What's important here?
14. what's really happening?
15. What matters most to you in this moment?
16. What do you believe about yourself in this situation?
17. Approach from different places..."What would your

heart say? What about your head/brain/ younger self / older self?"

18. What are the facts in this situation?

19. And then what? (What happens next in this scenario?)

20. What are you having a hard time believing because of who's sharing the information?

21. Are you listening to all contributors regardless of position / authority?

22. If you viewed things from another person's point of view, what new information would that perspective give you?

23. What if?

24. What would the other person (boss, partner, client) think?

25. What if you were flying above the situation?

26. What are you relying too heavily on? What have you anchored your opinion on?

27. How do you think the other person views the situation?

28. What would that look like next year?

TEAMS

1. What have you been doing automatically, which may need reexamined?
2. Who has recently done this task/project successfully/unsuccessfully and how can you learn from them?
3. Are you listening to all contributors regardless of position / authority?
4. How can you avoid discussing things you've already agreed on and move onto the difficult conversations?
5. What should you/your team do more of?
6. What should you/your team do less of?
7. What should your/your team start doing?
8. What should you/your team stop doing?
9. What should you/your team learn how to do?
10. What should you/your team be more open to?
11. What should you/your team be firm on?
12. In what team role do you feel most confident?

13. What do you spend too much time on that has little or no value?
14. Where are the bottlenecks in your business/process? Where is the work piled up?
15. How is sharing this information / opinion about someone else (who is not present) going to help them?
16. Who's impacted by this action?
17. What is it you're not seeing?
18. What unique contribution can you make?
19. What are you truly committed to?
20. What are you ready to commit to right now?
21. Who's impacted by this decision?
22. What resource is most at risk of running out?
23. What do you think they should know without me telling them? Is that reasonable?
24. How do you want them to behave differently?
25. Who on your team is overwhelmed?
26. Who is the most stressed on the team?
27. Who do you hear from the least?
28. Who do you hear from the most?
29. What's your preferred form of communication?
30. Do you have to be at this meeting or event?
31. What area / skill may you be at risk of thinking you're better than you actually are?
32. What area / skill may you be at risk of thinking you're worse than you actually are?
33. Who plays the supporting role to you as the hero? Who is your biggest fan?

VALUES

1. What energizes you?
2. What drains your energy?
3. What is really important to you - rather than merely urgent? What is your underlying purpose here?
4. If there were no constraints, what would you do? If you suspended doubt and worry, what action would you take?
5. What are you truly committed to?
6. What are you ready to commit to right now?
7. What do you really want - specifically?
8. What are the three most important elements of a life filled with joy?
9. What's the most important thing you learned from your parents?
10. What emotion do you most want to feel?
11. What emotion do you least want to feel?
12. What are your top three pet peeves?

13. What 5 items would you put on your bucket list?
14. Why do you work?
15. When was the last time you lost track of time? What were you doing at the time?
16. Where are you along your plan?

VISION

1. What 5 items would you put on your bucket list?
2. Where are you along your plan?
3. What type of things can you do to close the gap? Reduce the difference?
4. What's your vision of your professional future in 5 / 10 / 15 years?
5. What's your vision of your lifestyle in 5 / 10 / 15 years?
6. What will it take to make your vision a reality?
7. What do you need to know to turn your vision into reality?
8. What do you need to have done to turn your vision into reality?
9. What do you need to believe in order to turn your vision into reality?
10. What do you need to be doing 6 months / 1 year / 5 years before your vision becomes a reality?
11. What would you do if you knew you could not fail?
12. What's your biggest hope or dream?

13. What bothers you most in the world?
14. If you could go back and talk to your younger self, what would you like her/him to know?
15. What's missing from this picture so far?
16. What unique contribution can you make?
17. What is the better version of you?
18. How would you rate / describe your satisfaction with respect to: family? Is that what you want? If not, what do you want to be different here?
19. How would you rate / describe your satisfaction with respect to: friends/social? Is that what you want? If not, what do you want to be different here?
20. How would you rate / describe your satisfaction with respect to: work? Is that what you want? If not, what do you want to be different here?
21. How would you rate / describe your satisfaction with respect to: health? Is that what you want? If not, what do you want to be different here?
22. How would you rate / describe your satisfaction with respect to: spirituality? Is that what you want? If not, what do you want to be different here?
23. How would you rate / describe your satisfaction with respect to: finances? Is that what you want? If not, what do you want to be different here?
24. What things do you like or dislike in each area of your life/business?
25. What are you doing now to shape your life tomorrow?

PART III
A FEW EXTRAS

Sometimes questions are just for fun. This section has two additional lists of a different sort of question.

THE PIVOT QUESTIONS

These 10 questions originally came from a French series, "Bouillon de Culture" hosted by Bernard Pivot. They're better known as the questions James Lipton asks every guest during his famous program "Inside the Actor's Studio."

Answer the questions yourself. Have fun with friends. Use them at an event or team building (when appropriate.)

You'll be amazed at how much they reveal about a person's thoughts, feelings and beliefs.

1. What is your favorite word?
2. What is your least favorite word?
3. What turns you on creatively, spiritually or emotionally?
4. What turns you off creatively, spiritually or emotionally?
5. What sound or noise do you love?
6. What sound or noise do you hate?
7. What is your favorite curse word? (stars with pre and post indicators will suffice)

8. What profession other than your own would you like to attempt?

9. What profession would you not like to do?

10. If Heaven exists, what would you like to hear God say when you arrive at the Pearly Gates?

QUESTIONS FOR TABLE DISCUSSIONS

*C*onversations around the table can result in amazing shifts in perspective, innovative ideas, life changing relationships, and team building connections. Here are a few questions to ask everyone at the table to answer.

1. If we're sitting here a year from now celebrating something huge, what would it be?
2. What's the best creative advice you've ever been given?
3. If you could have one do-over, what would it be?
4. What's a habit you're trying to adopt right now?
5. Who did you make a genuine connection with today?

THANK YOU

TWO BONUSES JUST FOR YOU

Two bonuses to help you leap forward on your journey to

Get your ideas out of your head and into the world!

BONUS #1: POWERFUL QUESTIONS WORKSHOP.

A short but powerful **audio program** designed to bring the experience of executive coaching to you where and when you need a boost.

BONUS #2: EXECUTIVE COACH'S BONUS QUESTIONS.

These **follow-up questions** are used to dig deeper and overcome blocks that often appear when you ask a difficult question.

Get started: lindadeluca.net/start/

YOUR QUESTIONS, ANSWERED

Thank you for exploring the ultimate actionable strategy of powerful questions. I hope you continue use these and other questions to discover, influence, inspire, and grow your business and yourself.

If you loved the book and have a moment to spare, I would really appreciate a short review on the site where you purchased. Your help in spreading the word is gratefully received!

Do you have a question you'd like to ask me? Please reach out: lindadeluca.net/contact and you'll get answers!

ABOUT THE AUTHOR

LINDA DELUCA

Coach | Author | Entrepreneur

In 2007, after years of working in corporate as an employee, I chose to become an independent consultant and work remotely. With that decision came an exciting journey complete with obstacles, restrictions, excitement, opportunities and learning, learning and more learning.

I discovered the definition of work was changing and the future of work requires a different set of skills. Because I have such a love of learning, I set out to discover, develop, and share those unique requirements for successfully working remotely and independently.

Over the years I've designed and developed numerous workshops and written books and articles focusing on actionable strategies to help you and I delivery our best work. This series is part of that body of work.

With more than 25 years of business experience in executing a multitude of functions across diverse industries, you could say I've studied at the school of life. That along with my formal education in business and organizational development has provided me with invaluable knowledge (and wisdom).

With a mix of process design, business acumen, love of technology and curiosity about human behavior, I bring a unique perspective to my projects and in helping my clients.

For more information visit
www.lindadeluca.net

Find more resources for getting your ideas and your brilliance out of your head and into the world at LindaDeLuca.net

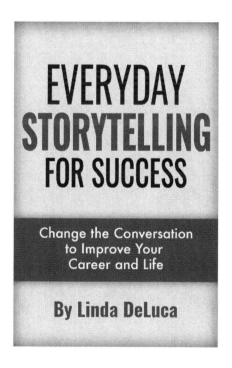

EVERYDAY STORYTELLING FOR SUCCESS

Change the Conversation to Improve Your Career and Life

You don't need to be a keynote speaker to be a good storyteller.

No matter where you are in your career, the odds are high that you need to influence your peers, your boss, or your customers, to achieve your desired success. Storytelling is neither natural for everyone nor actively taught in schools or business training programs. Everyday Storytelling for Success fills that void.

This book is full of practical approaches to using storytelling that can be applied by anyone. The book combines not only the reasoning why and where storytelling will help you achieve your desired business results, but more importantly it provides step-by-step guide to using storytelling everyday in your professional life whether you are looking for work, getting to work, or leading others in work.

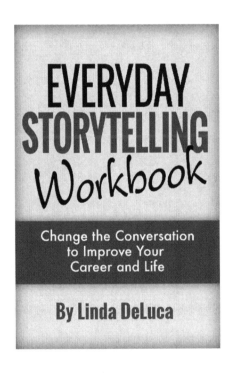

EVERYDAY
STORYTELLING
Workbook

Change the Conversation
to Improve Your
Career and Life

By Linda DeLuca

EVERYDAY STORYTELLING WORKBOOK

A blend of leadership development, communication strategy, and executive coaching, Everyday Storytelling Workbook is the perfect companion to Everyday Storytelling For Success and guides you to change your conversations, build trust, and connect with those important to your success.

This workbook is a hands-on guide of discovery, craft, and practice of storytelling by experimenting with both small daily changes and deep dive challenges all working toward mastering the skills of connecting to and inspiring others through powerful storytelling.

———————